TEEN LEADERSHIP

networking guidebook

A **net** worlding LEADERSHIP SERIES BOOK

net worlding
PUBLISHING
Books and more that make the world better!

ISBN 978-0-9838128-4-5

Copyright © 2001 by Networlding– All Rights Reserved.

This document is adapted with permission from materials contained in Networlding: Building Relationships and Opportunities for Success in the New Networked Economy Guidebook by Melissa Giovagnoli and Jocelyn Carter-Miller; copyrighted text and data from these sources are used in this document in their original form and format.

Networlding Publishing
www.networlding.com

Special acknowledgements for additional contributions:

Thank you, Jon Malysiak, for your additional insights and content that go a long way toward helping the teenage reader see the relevance of Networlding and the importance of building social networks in their young lives.

Table of Contents

NetWorlding Overview and Introduction

"Networlding is a long journey rather than a short ride, and you want to make sure that those you share it with are people you truly feel connected to on a deeper level than money. The journey must be marked not only by your continuous success but by the success of others."

(NETWORLDING P. 37)

What is *NetWorlding*™?

Networlding™ is all about making meaningful connections and leveraging those connections in new and powerful ways. As teenagers—whether you are currently in high school, starting your college careers, or looking for your first job—you are in a position to start laying the foundation for your life in the adult world. Now is really the time to start thinking about making connections with the people who are going to help you both now and in the future. Life is all about building meaningful connections, and the more of these you have now, the easier it will be for you to fulfill your dreams and live the life you have always imagined. Having a great education is only part of the process. The people you meet now—in school, on your sports teams and your extra-curricular activities, in your places of worship—are the ones who are going to open doors for you in the future in ways that you may not even imagine.

Think about a map. A map guides you. It shows you what you need to know to get where you want to be – your path is laid out for you. A map is a useful tool that allows you to control your journey. **Networlding**™ is your map to help jump-start your networking process AND put you in the driver's seat and get you where you want to be.

Networlding™ is a unique, accelerated networking program. It goes deeper than traditional networking because it creates an entire support system that includes not only people who can help you in the short term, but people who understand your goals, share your values, and provide shared support and benefits, time and time again. It also gives you, and lets you offer others, a sense of accomplishment in the process.

In this ever-advancing world it seems that we have new communication tools available to us everyday. Tools like email and Facebook make it easier to connect with others.

To take full advantage of this new age, we need to understand how we are all connected and how we can use these connections to benefit everyone involved. We also need to change our ideas of what it takes to succeed in our personal relationships, in school, in college, and on a job. This means shifting from a "me" perspective to a "we" perspective, and it means forming lasting relationships in totally different ways.

Networlding™ is the strategy that allows you to look past the opportunities, to see the people who can help you take advantage of those opportunities . . . to think of your relationships not as pipelines to opportunities, but as lifelines in a more connected world.

With **Networlding**™ everyone involved is compelled to help each other succeed as well as grow, get results as well as learn, and achieve goals as well as become empowered. This guidebook, and the **Networlding**™ text, along with the other participants will get you connected to the seven steps of Networlding and a group to help you move through the process.

Remember, this is <u>your</u> map ... let it guide you where you want to go.

Here is the Power-of-Ten **Networlding**™ journey.

NetWorlding™ vs. networking

Networlding	Networking
Value-based	Goal-based
Leveraged learning	Double the effort
Long-term commitment	Temporary
Relational	Transactional
Conscious, strategic process	Haphazard process
Benefits all involved	Often one-sided
Organized	Disorganized
Holistic	Often Materialistic
Intimate	Superficial
Opportunity Expansive	Opportunity Specific
Multi-dimensional	Two-dimensional
Networlding relationships start when you clearly express your intent. Quickly and convincingly, you explain your goals and values, and when you do so, people who feel the same way will respond. If someone responds positively and you are able to establish a Networlding relationship, you can reap tremendous benefits. Your new partner will not only do more for you in terms of opportunities but in providing an empathetic ear and a source of fresh ideas.	In contrast, **networking** connections are flimsy because they lack support. When networking, people are bound together because one person needs another to accomplish something, but isn't concerned with returning the favor. One particular situation binds them together, and as soon as this situation disintegrates or disappears, there's nothing left of the relationship to keep it strong enough to survive.

What You Will Need:

1. A Letter of Commitment

2. The book, Networlding: Building Relationships and Opportunities for Success, the conceptual backbone of this process and this Guidebook to keep you on track.

3. A Journal to capture free thinking, ideas, success stories, stumbling blocks, and inspirations, or use the journal pages provided with this guidebook.

The NetWorlding "Community of Practice"

In this workshop we will be covering all the steps of a seven-step **Networlding**™ process. You will be asked to perform exercises for each step of the process. Some of the exercises you will do on your own and others will be done with people in this "Power-of-Ten Circle". The **seven steps are outlined** in the chart below along with the **day's agenda** from our website, www.networlding.com.

Step No. or Title	Description	Times
Registration	Roster Check-in, Name Tags & Tent Cards.	7:30a.m.
	BREAKFAST	8:00a.m.
Networlding Preview	Networlding vs. networking	8:00-9:45a.m.
	BREAK	9:45-10:15a.m.
STEP One: Establish a Values-Rich Foundation	Take the Quiz. Identify your top values. Discover linkages to family and school values and goals. Begin completing your Circle profile.	10:15a.m.
STEP Two: Make Connections for Your Primary Circle	Identify who is currently in your Primary Circle and why.	

Step No. or Title	Description	Times
STEP Three: **Expand Your Circles**	Identify and connect with new people who have similar and complimentary values.	12:15p.m.
STEP Four: **Initiate Exchanging** **Relationships**	*LUNCH*	12:15-1:15p.m.
	Develop relationships more effectively by finding out what matters to others.	
STEP Five: **Grow and Nurture** **Relationships**	Develop relationships with Primary Networlding Partners using The Networlding Support Exchange Model	1:15p.m.
STEP Six: **Co-create Opportunities**	Create transformational opportunities through continuous exchanges	3:15p.m.
	BREAK	3:15-3:30p.m.
STEP Seven: **Recreate Your NetWorld**	Achieve your goals: constantly reassess and expand relationships that align with your values.	3:30-4:30p.m.
Full Networlding Among **Circle Members**	Optional Exercises Chosen	4:30-5:00p.m.

Contract / Letter of Commitment

Networlding is about creating communities of support, built on trust, respect and well-being. It is a process of collaboration that achieves mutual goals and leads to personal and professional and personal fulfillment. This is the Age of the Relationship, where our relationships become one of our most critical assets. Networlding is based on a Seven-step process. The following is the commitment I make to this process:

- ✓ I agree to support my learning circle to start and end each session/segment on time.

- ✓ I agree to complete all assignments/exercises as they are due to be able to fully contribute to the conversation and to get the most out of the process.

- ✓ I agree that if I am dissatisfied with the experience or have concerns that I will seek a private conversation with the Facilitator in order to resolve.

- ✓ I agree to create a safe Networlding environment and commit to **confidentiality** so that people can feel safe really utilizing the group; I agree not to repeat anyone's challenges, confidences, or speak in any way that does not support the identity of group members outside of the meeting.

- ✓ I agree to contribute to the creation of an environment that supports everyone and gives opportunity for all to participate. I acknowledge that this is not therapy.

- ✓ I agree to be an active listener; listening more than I will talk. I will learn about individuals so that I may find ways to support them. I will be a giver with the intention of giving first and I will think exchange for mutual benefit.

- ✓ I agree to follow-up with those I have met via Networlding to learn more about them and what they care about, to explore what's possible for both of us. In addition, I will follow-up with others as I said I would and take and return calls if I agreed to talk later.

- ✓ I will honor my values and seek to develop relationships with people who share them. (This is a critical time saver.)

- ✓ I will be considerate of others' time constraints. I will include other people in conversations; if I am at an event I will look to include others.

- ✓ I agree that everyone's viewpoint is valid and will build on what has been said without criticism.

Take the Networlding Quiz

Questions	Never =1	Seldom =2	Occasionally =3	Often =4	Always =5
1. Believe it is important to make a difference					
2. Believe that anything is possible					
3. Believe you are guided by strong inner beliefs, intent or principles					
4. Believe you create your own rewards					
5. Believe you can get anything done through others					
6. Believe people are your most creative resource					
7. Share your goals with others					
8. Build/nurture relationships with those who can help you achieve your goals					
9. Limit relationships with selfish individuals and those that don't help you realize your goals					
10. Respect the creative process and are result/outcome focused					
11. Believe that Networlding/ Networking shortens the time to get things done					
12. Assume that Networlding/ Networking is a balanced process of giving and receiving					

Questions	Never =1	Seldom =2	Occasionally =3	Often =4	Always =5
13. Believe Networlding/ Networking can provide all needed resources to reach your goals					
14. When Networlding/ Networking you ask for what you want					
15. When Networlding/ Networking you discover others' interests and needs					
16. When Networlding/ Networking you expect to discover/create new opportunities					
17. Networld/ Network with influential people who can make things happen					
18. Offer emotional, information and other support to your Networld/ Network partners					
19. Respond quickly to the requests and needs of your Networld/ Network partners					
20. Measure the results of your Networlding/ Networking efforts					
TOTAL YOUR SCORE					

NOVICE (SCORE: 20-44), NETWORKER (SCORE: 45-64),
STRATEGIC NETWORKER (SCORE: 65-84), NETWORLDING EXPERT (SCORE: 85-100)

Establish a Values-Rich Foundation

"Try not to be a man of success, but rather a man of value".
(ALBERT EINSTEIN)

Before you can become well networked and collaborative, you need to identify your top values. These values live with you daily. They drive your behavior in school and at home and most of all they will help build a powerful network of people who hold similar and complementary values. These people who share your values will become your partners on the path to changing opportunities. For example, two people who value service might be a great match to work together on a community service project.

From the textbook: Chapters 1, 2 & 3

Networlding, Chapter 1, "What is Networlding, Anyway?" (pp. 1 –23) and Chapter 2, "Networlding Golden Rules" (pp. 24 – 36). Use the book as a resource during your **Networlding** journey.

Networlding, Chapter 3, "Step One: Establish a Values-Rich Foundation," (pp. 37-53).

Step #1 Exercise: Identify Your Top Values

Values are the principles that guide your actions on a daily basis. Becoming strongly aware of your values and creating goals that reflect those values builds a foundation for success. Living your personal and academic lives according to those values creates a feeling of authenticity in the way you present yourself. Being genuine inspires trust and confidence and leads to credibility.

Values clarification is both the first and final step in laying that foundation for success. If you **understand what is important to you and what drives you, you can match your actions with your values and increase the level of passion _and_ satisfaction in your life**.

Values clarification is also a necessary and important step in the transition from doing the things you are skilled at to doing the things you are passionate about. You can be good at a job, school project or task without being passionate about it. **When you identify an overlap between what motivates you and where you _excel_, you've found a passion!**

You'll know a school project, task, or job is a passion when it's easy, fun and time slips away because you are focused and having a good time! You will also want to share your achievements with your classmates, friends and peers because it is important to you and you will be passionate about what you've accomplished. In doing so, you may even inspire others to succeed as well.

You are at your most productive when you are passionate about a task or job. Being passionate and engaged allows you to better achieve your goals and objectives.

Achieving a top level of performance at school, at your job, or in your extra-curricular activities begins with you. As you identify the things that are important to you and find your passions, you create an environment that makes success possible. The first step is in this process is identifying your values.

In this exercise, you will identify and clarify your values. Once you establish your values and set your goals, you can then translate your goals into actions.

Values List

The following table lists many personal values, but is in no way intended to be complete. Feel free to use these, or add any others important to you, as you complete your pre-work.

Exercise:

1a) *Check off as many values as apply to you for today*

❏ Achievement	❏ Empowerment	❏ Making a Difference
❏ Advancement	❏ Fame	❏ Non-judgmental
❏ Adventure	❏ Family	❏ Order
❏ Affiliation	❏ Focus	❏ Personal Development
❏ Authority	❏ Freedom	❏ Pleasure
❏ Autonomy	❏ Friendship	❏ Power
❏ Balance	❏ Fun	❏ Quality
❏ Collaboration	❏ Giver	❏ Recognition
❏ Community	❏ Happiness	❏ Responsibility
❏ Competence	❏ Health	❏ Safety
❏ Competition	❏ Helpfulness	❏ Self Motivation
❏ Connection	❏ Honoring	❏ Self respect
❏ Contribution	❏ Inner Harmony	❏ Service
❏ Cooperation	❏ Integrity	❏ Spirituality
❏ Courage	❏ Involvement	❏ Success
❏ Creativity	❏ Knowing	❏ Trust
❏ Earning money	❏ Knowledge	❏ Wisdom
❏ Social connection	❏ Loyalty	

Note: All of the values listed are important. You are identifying what drives you. For example, do not feel compelled to select "family" as a value if it is not what motivates you to action. That does not mean you don't care for your family.

Values Selection:

1b) *You may partner with a member of your learning Circle to cull your list to 3 values, and write them on your "Power Strategy Guide" in the Appendix (p. 40).*

1c) *Be prepared to share your 3 values with the members of the group.*

Goal Creation

1d) *Create one corresponding goal that aligns with your values. Make sure your goals are S.M.A.R.T.: Specific, Measurable, Attainable, Results oriented and Time-bound. Share your goal and discuss which of your top 3 values apply. What strategies will you employ to achieve that goal?*

1e) *Pull out the "Power Strategy Guide" for the next Steps.*

Strategies For Leveraging Your Values

1. Share the three values you chose with a couple of people who know you very well (e.g., parents, peers, close friends, teachers, coaches, etc.) Ask them to identify what they believe are your top values—those values you demonstrate to them most often.

2. Do your chosen values and the ones they chose for you match? Remember, nothing is etched in stone. Your values may change over time. Different values will be more important to you at various stages of your life. There may be some values important to you in your academic life that differ from those important in your family life.

3. Did your values align with your current activities? What needs to change?

   For example, say your focus is your personal life and you choose as one of your top goals to secure a new key relationship or friendship. Let's also say that one of your top values is creativity. How can you use your value of creativity to help you achieve your goal?

NOTES

_____

_____

_____

_____

_____

_____

_____

_____

_____

_____

_____

_____

_____

_____

_____

_____

_____

_____

_____

_____

_____

_____

Your Circle Profile

1f) *Partner with a Circle member to complete your Circle Profile.*

NAME:		PRIMARY PHONE:	PRIMARY EMAIL:
Student ❑ Employed ❑		School	Grade
Area Of Interest			

Personal Skills & Responsibilities
Personal Values: *(What you value most in your personal and work relationships?)*

Personal Information Affecting Future Decisions
Personal Interests: *(What you do you for fun?)*

Supporting Others in Networlding
Help Others Connect: *(How you can help connect people to those they want to meet or create the opportunities they want to create?)*

The kinds of people or opportunities to be connected with
How would you like others to help or support you:

Your last great Networlding opportunity you created
The story about how you connected with someone and worked on an opportunity together:

Make Connections For Your Primary Circle

"Just ask yourself: To whom would I turn to get something done—someone who is strongly connected to two people or someone who is lightly connected to 150 people? Any doubts about your answer?"
(JAMES M. KOUZES – AUTHOR, THE LEADERSHIP CHALLENGE)

Like many people you may also want to find opportunities that are both fun and rewarding. To accomplish this you need to build networks or "Circles" that will draw on both your skills and interests. Step Two in the Networlding process involves the formation of your Primary Circle, a group of no more than five people, to start with, who hold complimentary values to yours and are ready, willing and able to start the process of Networlding with you.

Remember to choose contacts that are supportive, continuous communicators, reliable and responsible, influential, knowledgeable, are active listeners, empathic, appreciative, and connection conscious. These contacts may include a favorite teacher or tutor or coach, a school guidance or career counselor, someone from your worship community or anyone that you feel has a positive influence on your life.

From the textbook: Chapter 4

Networlding, Chapter 4, "Step 2: Make Connections for Your Primary Circle" (pp. 54-69).

Step #2 Exercise: Creating Your Primary Circle

You will be identifying potential members of your Primary Circle, and then narrowing down the list of potential members by assessing how each potential member's values would fit with your own. You will partner with a member of your learning Circle to help form your Primary Circle.

2a) *On your Networlding Power Strategy Guide in the Appendix (p.40), jot down a list of up to 10 people you know. Use the following list to help you.*

DOCTOR	RELATIVES	TEAMMATES
NON-PROFIT HEADS	FRIENDS OF FRIENDS	CLASSMATES
RESTAURANT OWNERS	FRIENDS PARENTS	TEACHERS/PROFESSORS
RELIGIOUS LEADERS	HAIRDRESSER	MUSIC INSTRUCTORS
POLITICANS	LIBRARIAN	GUIDANCE COUNSELOR
CURRENT EMPLOYERS	DENTIST	COACHES
GOVERNMENT DEPARTMENTS	PARENTS FRIENDS	EDITORS
ALUMNI	TUTORS	NEIGHBORS
PAST EMPLOYERS	SPEAKERS	PEOPLE IN PR
FRIENDS	RELATIVES	OTHER:

People I know who support the causes I support

_____

_____

_____

_____

_____

_____

_____

_____

People I know who participate in activities complementary to mine

_____

_____

_____

_____

_____

_____

_____

_____

2b) *Check off those people on the list whose values complement your own (if you're stuck here, review page 58 in Networlding).*

Notes:

_____

_____

_____

_____

_____

_____

_____

2c) *Partner up and Pare your Circle down to no more than five people <u>who may be ready, willing and able to Networld with you</u> over the course of the next 2 months. Even one person is sufficient to begin Networlding effectively. List your potential Primary Circle partners on your <u>Potential Partner Map</u> from the Appendix (p. 41).*

Notes:

_____

_____

_____

_____

_____

_____

_____

Share with your partner the one person you plan to connect up with before the next meeting to discuss their participation in your Primary Circle. Commit to meeting with this person to discuss the following:

- Your interest in having them in your Primary Circle.
- The Networlding process so far.
- Share your top values and their connection to your goals.
- A commitment to connecting with your partner at least once a month for the next two months to exchange information, knowledge, etc

_____

_____

_____

_____

_____

_____

2d) *Share with the full group your findings.*

Use the Potential Partner Map in the Appendix (p. 41). This worksheet combines your goal and values with those potential partners' goals and values to begin to round out your primary Circle from Exercises h) and i) above.

_____

_____

_____

_____

_____

_____

_____

Step #2 Exercise: Applying The Support Exchange Model

See the **Networlding™** Support Exchange Model below and "Leverage" example below

EXERCISE:

2e) *Use the Support Exchange Model as a tool to develop relationships with your primary Circle partners. Also examine the "Awareness, Recognition, Ownership, Leverage" example below*

Questions to Ask Primary Circle Participants:	
Ready	Do they have the time?
Willing	Can they commit to conversations once a month at least for an hour?
Able	Do they feel and think they have something to contribute?
	Do you use the Support Exchange Model?
	At every level of the Support Exchange Model ask: "What matters most?"

Awareness Identify someone who could be a potential primary Circle partner .

Recognition Have a conversation. Discuss your value or values. Inquire about theirs. Move through a conversation that focuses upon the seven levels of support.

Ownership The potential partner becomes a partner. You practice the seven levels of support in structured meetings. (Note: we recommend you exchange the first and second meetings face-to-face. After that, you can connect by phone and / or email.)

Leverage You have ongoing conscious conversations.

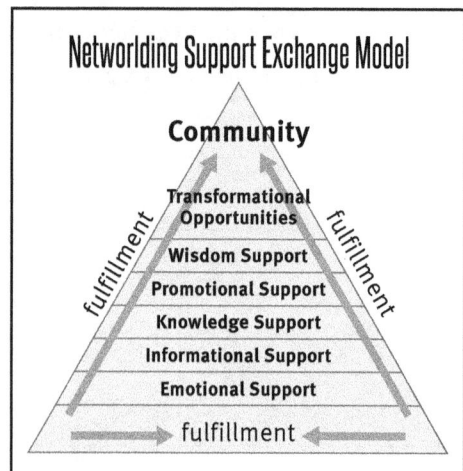

Networlding Support Exchange Model

Community

Transformational Opportunities

Wisdom Support

Promotional Support

Knowledge Support

Informational Support

Emotional Support

fulfillment

STEP THREE
Expand Your Circles

"Reality lies in how you see things".
(PABLO PICASSO)

Once you have reviewed your current network and identified five or fewer key connections for your Primary Circle, you can begin to fill in the gaps in your Circle so that you have a rich, diverse base of connections that will help pursue your goals. Anyone who is important to achieving your goals should be considered.

Growing your Primary Circle is a fun, exciting process that, even with a little effort, will result in great success for you!

You can find influencers through many different pathways such as

- The Internet
- Periodicals
- Conferences and lectures
- School organizations and associations

- Through Volunteering
- Committees
- Lists, Directories, Alumni groups
- When traveling

- Through leisure activities
- Through people who know people that you know

From the textbook: Chapter 5

Networlding, Chapter 5, "Step 3: Expand Your Circles," (pp. 70-101) as a complement to the **Networlding** process.

Step #3 Exercise: Expanding Your Circle

In this exercise, you will focus on the expansion of your Primary Circle. You will begin by reflecting on your reading from the book and developing a description of those people who would be good partners for you to exchange.

Potential Partner Map

3a) *First, think about your values; think about the 5 potential members of your Primary Circle from the last exercise; imagine the ideal mix of people you would want. Avoid editing yourself; let your ideas and imagination flow. Jot down your wish list on your Power Strategy Guide (p. 40). You can update the Potential Partner Map in the Appendix (p. 41) with your final list.*

3b) *Think of three people who might have a broad base of knowledge and influence—people who are ready, willing and able to partner with you. Who, because of that, would extend your Primary Circle. Write down their names and some information as to why they would make good Primary Circle partners.*

_____

_____

_____

_____

_____

_____

_____

_____

_____

_____

3c) *Be prepared to discuss these 2 lists (Primary Circle partners and extended / stretch partners) from your <u>Potential Partner Map</u> with the Group.*

Strategies for Leveraging Expanding Circles

4. Write down three high-profile people with whom you would enjoy speaking. Find out their contact information and <u>write it down later</u>. **This is List 1.**

5. Determine what groups you might want to belong to and write down their names and contact information. Consider both personal and professional organizations like community groups, school clubs, charities etc. **This is list 2.**

6. In the coming days choose someone from your lists in 1 and 2 above and have a conversation with them about your Networlding goals. Write down the benefits that you can offer this person. (Use the <u>Value, Goal, Strategy Maps</u> from the Appendix (pp. 49-50], for notes and preparation for conversations with these potential partners.)

_____

_____

_____

_____

_____

_____

_____

_____

_____

Feeling uneasy? Relax. Record your experience in the journal section of your guidebook. Remember, you are on a journey.

OPTIONAL EXERCISE: Benefits you can offer – Value, Goal, Strategy Maps

3d) *Discuss one potential Primary Circle contact with a learning Circle partner. Write the person's first name in the lines below. Write down the benefits you can offer this person (see The Support Exchange Model again).*

_____

_____

_____

_____

_____

_____

_____

_____

_____

You may transfer this information to one of the Circles in the Value, Goal, Strategy Maps from the Appendix (pp. 49-50].

Networlding Support Exchange Model

Community

Transformational Opportunities

Wisdom Support

Promotional Support

Knowledge Support

Informational Support

Emotional Support

fulfillment *fulfillment*

fulfillment

NOTES

_____

_____

_____

_____

_____

_____

_____

_____

_____

_____

_____

_____

_____

_____

_____

_____

_____

_____

_____

_____

_____

STEP FOUR
Initiate Exchanging Relationships

*"See things as you would have them be, instead
of as they are." (Robert Collier)*

Now that you have continued to develop your Primary Circle, it's time to prepare for ongoing conversations. Initiating exchanging relationships is a critical skill in today's connected society where you will need to form quick, meaningful relationships with people with whom you will partner for opportunities.

Identify top points of commonality- It's important to find things that you have in common with others. For example: dancing, sports, writing, favorite classes, volunteering, music, etc.

From the textbook: Chapter 6
Networlding, Chapter 6, "Step 4: Initiate Exchanging Relationships," (pp. 102-126).

Step #4 Exercise: Initiating a Support Exchange

Initiate a conversation with one person in your Circle using the Networlding Support Exchange Model where you focus on first creating an emotional connection. For example, a conversation might start, "Hello Joe, Julia told me you are in Advanced English. I enjoy writing articles for the school paper. What do you enjoy writing about?"

Review the *Support Exchange Conversation Maps* in the Appendix (pp. 42-48).

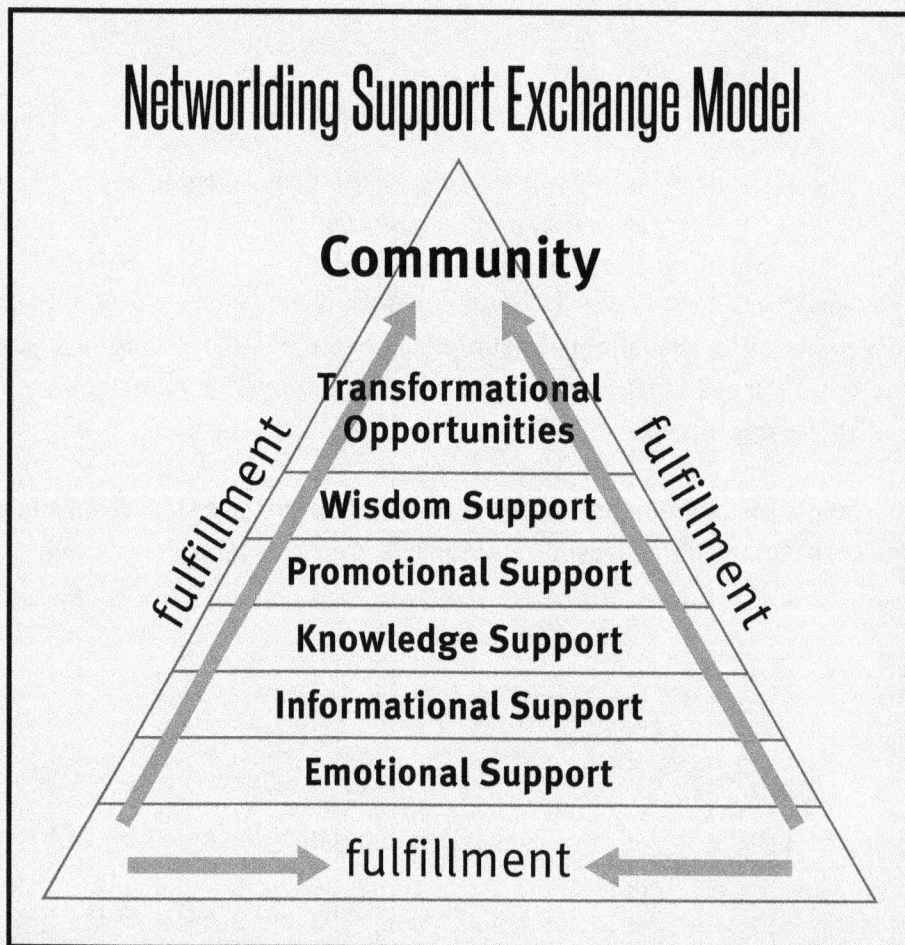

Networlding Support Exchange Model

Community

fulfillment

fulfillment

Transformational Opportunities

Wisdom Support

Promotional Support

Knowledge Support

Informational Support

Emotional Support

fulfillment

4a) *Partner with a learning Circle member and begin a support exchange conversation. Pretend that you have just met this person. Use your Power Strategy Guide (p.40).*

4b) *Spend 5 minutes each in the conversation.*

1. _____

_____

_____

_____

_____

2. _____

_____

_____

_____

_____

3. _____

_____

_____

_____

_____

4. _____

_____

_____

_____

_____

5. _____

_____

_____

_____

_____

6. _____

_____

_____

_____

_____

7. _____

_____

_____

_____

_____

OPTIONAL EXERCISE: Creating powerful relationships through conscious conversations.

4c) *Share with the Group your observations and impressions from the last exercise.*

List the one best question from each level of the Exchange Model.

1. _____

2. _____

3. _____

4. _____

5. _____

6. _____

7. _____

What specific actions can you take to incorporate what you have learned in this Step into your Networlding goals and strategies for your primary Circle members?

_____

_____

_____

_____

_____

_____

_____

_____

_____

Grow and Nurture Relationships – Maintaining and Deepening Existing Relationships

"Ah, that a man's reach should exceed his grasp, or what's a heaven for."
(ROBERT BROWNING)

You have created your values foundation, aligned your goals with your values, attached your values to action strategies and started Networlding partnerships with existing and new influential people. Now you will put your Primary Circle to use in order to create opportunities for yourself and your partners. Having regular conversations with your partners can accomplish this. Having a vision that reflects your value(s) and is associated with value statements leads to conscious and meaningful conversations.

From the textbook: Chapter 7

Networlding, Chapter 7, " Step 5: Grow and Nurture Relationships" (pp. 127-148) as a complement to the **Networlding** process.

Step #5 Exercises: Create Your Value Proposition & Vision Map

In this exercise you take a top value, and your one-year vision, to create a map of those value-proposition (VP) statements. *"VP" statements are the skills and experience that you bring to the success of your vision*. For example, your personal accomplishments and results; your ability to serve as an example; your trustworthiness; your credibility; the sense of unity, direction and purpose that you can provide; your unique perspective; the reference point you create, which will be an ongoing focus; the skills you can pass on; your singular knowledge or approaches; your talents, or your reputation.

Two people with a similar vision and complementary values will have different VP statements because of the skills and experiences they bring to relationships.

EXERCISE: Your Vision and Value Proposition Statements

5a) *Write your one-year vision in the space provided on the <u>Value Proposition & Vision Map</u> in the Appendix (p. 51). What top value will you focus on to achieve it? Write it down in the center of the map.*

5b) *Think about your value proposition. In other words, what makes you unique? Jot some ideas below. For example, "I am a good listener; I have great analytical skills, I am a great writer; I build strong relationships with others," etc.*

_____

_____

_____

_____

_____

_____

_____

_____

5c) <u>Using the *Value Proposition & Vision Map* write as many Value Propositions (what is unique about you) VP statements, one in each Circle (and add more Circles as needed) *Value Proposition & Vision Map* in the Appendix (p. 51).*</u>

5d) *We will either transfer the information from your Map to flip-chart paper and tape it to the wall, or put the form at your place at the table. In either case everyone will be able to reflect on your efforts and provide feedback.*

OPTIONAL EXERCISE: Present Your Map

Each person or volunteer(s) may present their <u>Value Proposition & Vision Map</u> to the whole Group.

5e) *Go around and all participants offer insights and support on each other's maps.*
- Share, using the Support Exchange Model as a guide.
- Note the value propositions you bring to take your relationships to a deeper level.
- Explore and talk about things you will share that you have in common—similar/complementary values.
- Discuss potential mutual opportunities you have.
- Ask your Circle partner to share the same.
- Make plans for another conversation within the next week.

_____

_____

_____

_____

_____

_____

_____

_____

_____

OPTIONAL EXERCISE: Deepen Your Relationships through Conversations

You will partner and use the <u>Support Exchange Conversation Maps</u> in the Appendix (pp. 42-48] and the <u>Potential Partner Map</u> in the Appendix (p. 41].

5f) *Think about your goal, vision and value propositions. What were the highlights of your last exercise exchange that you will use to <u>leverage relationships</u> in the development of your Primary Circle?*

Use the <u>Support Exchange Conversation</u> and <u>Potential Partner Maps</u> for notes.

Use the "Awareness, Recognition, Ownership, Leverage" paradigm below

Questions to Ask Primary Circle Participants:	
Ready	Do they have the time?
Willing	Can they commit to conversations once a month at least for an hour?
Able	Do they feel and think they have something to contribute?
	At every level of the Support Exchange Model ask: "What matters most?"

_____

_____

_____

_____

_____

_____

_____

_____

Networlding Support Exchange Model

Community

Transformational Opportunities

Wisdom Support

Promotional Support

Knowledge Support

Informational Support

Emotional Support

fulfillment

_____

_____

_____

_____

_____

_____

_____

_____

Awareness	Recognition
Identify someone who could be a potential primary Circle partner .	Have a conversation. Discuss your value or values. Inquire about theirs. Move through a conversation that focuses upon the seven levels of support.
Ownership	**Leverage**
The potential partner becomes a partner. You practice the seven levels of support in structured meetings. (Note: we recommend you exchange the first and second meetings face-to-face. After that, you can connect by phone and / or email.)	You have ongoing conscious conversations.

OPTIONAL EXERCISE: Maintaining and Deepening Existing Relationships

In this exercise you will review your <u>Value, Goal, Strategy Maps</u> from the Appendix (pp. 49-50]. Pull these pages out and have it in front of you.

5g) *What specific actions can you take to incorporate what you have learned in this Step into your Networlding goals and strategies?*

Have a full Group discussion.

_____

_____

_____

_____

_____

_____

_____

_____

_____

_____

_____

_____

_____

_____

_____

STEP SIX
Co-create Opportunities

"Do not dismiss any encounter as insignificant."
(JOHN HEADER — THE TAO OF LEADERSHIP)

How can you best create transformational opportunities? Sometimes you're so focused on your school obligations that you fail to take the time to create, or co-create with your Networlding partners, opportunities that could benefit you and your future in powerful, unique ways. You can achieve your goals much faster if you brainstorm with your Networlding partners. In addition, your partners can help you find things you didn't know existed, and enable you to avoid roadblocks and obstacles to success.

From the textbook: Chapter 8

Networlding, Chapter 8, "Step 6: Co-create Opportunities," (pp. 149 – 170).

Step #6 Exercises: Developing an Opportunity

EXERCISE: Group Discussion – Starting Exchanges and Supporting Each Other

- How do you start your exchange(s) with your Networlding partner(s)?
- How do you develop trust?

    For example, what things do you offer for support?

    What do your Networlding partner(s) offer?
- What obstacles do you see stopping you from having a successful exchange?
- How can you support your other team player's perceived obstacles (role playing, attending networking events together, etc.)?
- What best practices can you and your group identify that will help build better relationships with Networlding partners?

OPTIONAL EXERCISE: Co-creation Opportunity Questions

In this exercise partner with one person in your Learning Circle and have a conversation designed to find ways to help one another achieve your goals and even co-create opportunities. Refer to the Values, Goal, Strategy Maps from the Appendix (pp. 49-50).

6a)   *Answers to the following questions leads to co-creation opportunities.*

1. What are the greatest challenges/trends impacting you today?

_____

_____

_____

_____

_____

_____

_____

_____

_____

_____

_____

_____

_____

_____

_____

_____

_____

_____

_____

_____

_____

2. In the next year, what are the greatest opportunities you have for growth?

_____

_____

_____

_____

_____

_____

_____

_____

_____

_____

_____

_____

_____

_____

_____

_____

_____

_____

_____

3. What can we do for one another within the next couple of weeks that will help each of us moves closer to realizing our goals?

_____

_____

_____

_____

_____

_____

_____

_____

_____

_____

_____

_____

_____

_____

_____

_____

_____

_____

_____

4. Share information on one project or opportunity you are currently working on and ask for new ideas to have better success. Think about and record this helpful information.

_____

_____

_____

_____

_____

_____

_____

_____

_____

_____

_____

_____

_____

_____

_____

_____

_____

_____

_____

5. Is there a way to create a co-opportunity here? If so what might it look like?

_____

_____

_____

_____

_____

_____

_____

_____

_____

_____

_____

_____

_____

_____

_____

_____

_____

_____

_____

_____

STEP SEVEN
Recreate Your NetWorld

"If we think we can do it on our own today, we are sadly mistaken."
(JACK WELCH)

Step seven is really about the constant evaluation and practice of building your Networld. This practice will make Networlding a part of your everyday life. Additional coaching of the process, which is what you are about to experience, will help you make Networlding a highly conscious skill, helping you leverage your ability to communicate ideas quickly and effectively. This will lead too fast action in strategies critical to success. In the process you will find yourself living a happier, balanced life where your ideas are listened to and understood.

From the textbook: Chapters 9 & 10

Networlding, Chapter 9, " Step 7: Re-create Your Networld" (pp. 171-190) and Chapter 10, "Thriving in the Networlding Universe" (pp. 191-202) as a complement to the **Networlding** process.

Step #7 Exercises: Re-creating Your Networld

OPTIONAL EXERCISE: Making the Process Easier

7a) *Discuss your experiences and wisdom gained since the last step.*

- How difficult or easy do you think it will be to recreate your Networld?
- How can you use your values to recreate your Networld?
- What best practice can you identify to recreate your Networld?

_____

_____

_____

_____

_____

_____

_____

_____

_____

_____

_____

_____

_____

_____

_____

_____

_____

EXERCISE: Take the Networlding Quiz again.
Discuss how you perceive your Networlding competence now.

Take the Networlding Quiz	Never =1	Seldom =2	Occasionally =3	Often =4	Always =5
1. Believe it is important to make a difference					
2. Believe that anything is possible					
3. Believe you are guided by strong inner beliefs, intent or principles					
4. Believe you create your own rewards					
5. Believe you can get anything done through others					
6. Believe people are your most creative resource					
7. Share your goals with others					
8. Build/nurture relationships with those who can help you achieve your goals					
9. Limit relationships with selfish individuals and those that don't help you realize your goals					
10. Respect the creative process and are result/outcome focused					
11. Believe that Networlding/ Networking shortens the time to get things done					

12. Assume that Networlding/ Networking is a balanced process of giving and receiving					
13. Believe Networlding/ Networking can provide all needed resources to reach your goals					
14. When Networlding/ Networking you ask for what you want					
15. When Networlding/ Networking you discover others' interests and needs					
16. When Networlding/ Networking you expect to discover/create new opportunities					
17. Networld/ Network with influential people who can make things happen					
18. Offer emotional, information and other support to your Networld/ Network partners					
19. Respond quickly to the requests and needs of your Networld/ Network partners					
20. Measure the results of your Networlding/ Networking efforts					
Total Your Score NOW					

NOVICE (SCORE: 20-44), NETWORKER (SCORE: 45-64),
STRATEGIC NETWORKER (SCORE: 65-84), NETWORLDING EXPERT (SCORE: 85-100)

OPTIONAL EXERCISE: Reviewing Your Commitment to The Networlding Process.

In this final set of exercises, review your learning and results from the previous six steps. A key element of these exercises is adding your learnings to your collective knowledge base. Do this by creating a summary of your success stories and best practices to be turned in at the group meeting.

7b) *Review your journal and identify key lessons. Make notes here:*

_____

_____

_____

_____

_____

_____

_____

7c) *What new opportunities have you generated at the completion of this course? Make notes here:*

_____

_____

_____

_____

_____

_____

_____

_____

7d) *Discuss what more you can be doing to support your Primary Circle partners' goals to achieve success and what further support you can ask for to achieve your goals.*

_____

_____

_____

_____

_____

_____

_____

_____

7e) *Now that you have completed this course what will you do to lead another circle of learning and peer mentor?*

_____

_____

_____

_____

_____

_____

_____

_____

APPENDIX A
Networlding Lexicon

Networlding is a seven-step process that helps you build trusting, satisfying and empowering relationships faster. Leaders growing their organizations, relationships or careers experience the creation of transformational opportunities.

Community Circles, Circles, Power-of-Ten Circles, Core Circles, Community Learning Circles, Career Learning Circles   Power-of-Ten Circles are practice Circles of ten or fewer people who gather to learn and practice the seven steps of Networlding. These Circles can be created by you or with support from those continuously signing up to join Networlding Circles all over the world.

Creating a Values Foundation   To get on the path toward establishing your values foundation, take these six actions

- Decide what matters to you most
- Identify your values priorities
- Align your values with your actions
- Create a personal charter
- Set goals
- Establish a one-year plan

Create a Personal Charter   A charter is your mandate to act, an overarching statement that describes who you want to be, what you want to do, the profession or principle to which you want to dedicate your life, and the legacy you want to leave.

Discernment   The key to understanding Networlding Connections. It is a meaningful connection based on an assessment of a potential relationship based on what is exchanged.

Horizon of Observability   The expanded focus of identifying your contacts holistically. This is the foreseeable number of people connected to those whom you meet.

Influencers   Those people of your Primary Circle who have the ability to influence other people and their actions. It is not a passive or titled-based concept, at least in the networld sense.

Influential Networlders   The kinds of behavior exhibited by networlders that might not be automatically associated with people of influence.

- Willingness to Give
- Community Involvement
- Awareness of Other's Needs and Interests
- Dependability
- Persistence
- Covisioning

"Learning Circle"   In a "Learning Circle" you focus on Networlding as a seven-step process that helps build trusting, satisfying and empowering relationships faster. Leaders growing their organizations, businesses, individuals in job search or career transition can focus on a "Learning Circle" experience to create the transformational opportunities. This happens through an exclusive Exchange Support Model.

Networlding   Networlding is, at its heart, a fun experience. People talk about their unique personal passions. That's what gets us up every morning. We also find most of the groups turn into friendship Circles. They end up setting up picnics, parties and special outings. We are also adding Networlding Dinners where Networlding members get the change to experience community and create new opportunities for their careers and businesses at the same time

Networlders' Beliefs   Although networlders' values are often different, their beliefs are usually similar. They create a "community of faith," people who adhere to the same tenets of success, purpose, and process.

Networlding Beliefs The beliefs that evolve over time which provide links to other networlders. They will inspire and motivate you, helping you move towards your goals. They are:

- Anything is possible with the support of others.
- It is important to make a difference.
- You get what you ask for.
- All resources will be provided to reach your goals.
- Life is filled with abundance and opportunities.
- There must be mutual rewards for partners.

Networlding Traits The following traits to help identify a good networlder as well as to help you become familiar with the traits you need to develop in yourself. The traits are:

- Supportive
- Continuous Communicators
- Reliable and Responsible
- Influential
- Knowledgeable
- Active Listener
- Empathic
- Appreciative
- Connection-Conscious

Power-of-Ten Extended Circle Once you join Networlding your Networlding Power-of-Ten Extended Circle is created after going through the Networlding "Learning Steps". After the five sessions and from any other Circles you choose to join at no extra charge.

Primary Circle The Circle that you interact with the most frequently. They are the combination personal think tank and pit team, offering encouragement, information and ideas in achieving what is most important to you. They are members who share traits of networlders, share your values and are influencers. You meet with them one on one and peer mentor with one another.

Structured Exchange Extensive studies on human networks show that you achieve better results (more connections, ongoing creativity, better opportunities) when you have regular (at least monthly) communications (we call them Exchanges) with a small, diverse group of people. Through the Power-of-Ten Circles, we will show you how to build a powerful Circle of people who can bring new and fresh perspectives to your business or career growth and for whom you can do the same.

Support Exchange Model

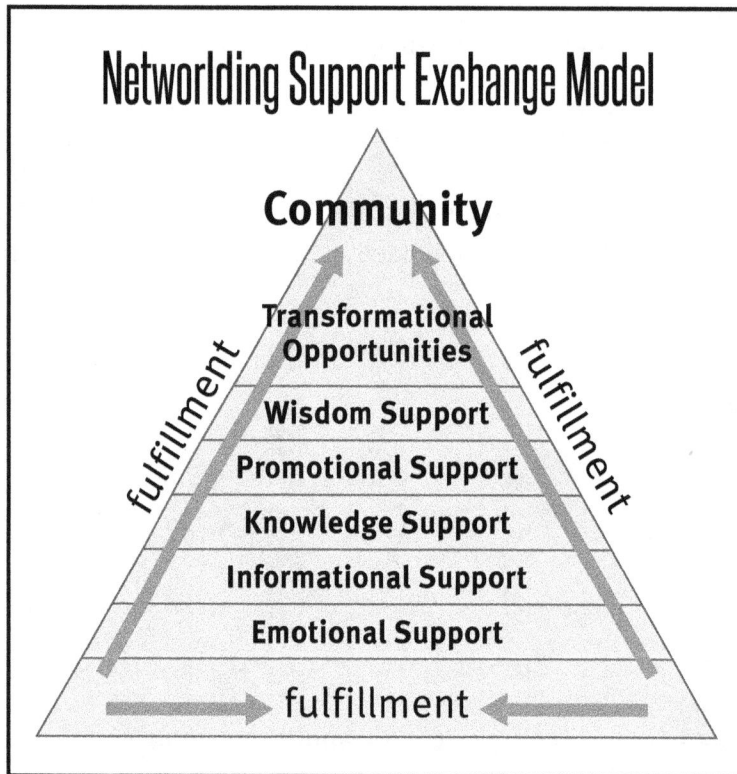

Networlding Support Exchange Model

Community

Transformational Opportunities

Wisdom Support

Promotional Support

Knowledge Support

Informational Support

Emotional Support

fulfillment

fulfillment

fulfillment

Building Personal and Professional Relationships

EXCERPTED FROM:

Networlding: Building Personal and Professional Relationships for Success in the New Connected Economy, by Melissa Giovagnoli and Jocelyn Carter Miller.

2000 The model illustrates the hierarchy of the development of relationships (like Maslow's Hierarchy of Needs for individuals) that evolves from a conscious communication exchange process with a select group of people.

Emotional Support: The part of consciousness that involves feelings. Our feelings about others serve as the foundations for our relationships. The focus of exchanging emotional support with another is to create rapport, a relationship of mutual trust and affinity.

Information Support: Information is a combination of messages. Once there is an initial rapport built, we then feel comfortable to share information of value.

Knowledge Support: Here, we add the element of experience. By sharing our personal experiences and those experiences of others we have heard, we add an additional value to our exchanges with others.

Promotional Support: As we continue to build rapport we naturally share with others the attributes of those whom we value. We heighten the awareness of these networlding partners to others and in doing so, better position them opportunities that arise.

Wisdom Support: Wisdom adds an element of time, clarity and understanding to our communications with others. Wisdom also adds the element of caring and compassion—a real desire to help others develop and achieve their life's dreams.

Transformational Opportunities: A natural result of emotional, informational, knowledge, promotional and wisdom support is a favorable or advantageous combination of circumstances. Opportunities can be leads or referrals or new jobs or business, personal or professional. The Networlding Exchange creates opportunities we can actually see evolving.

Community: This support results from a series of exchanges. A critical mass is reached when two or more people consciously connect regularly to support one another. There is a ripple effect that occurs as each party to a networlding relationship shares various forms of support with others in his or her community and it is further shared and so on. If you change yourselves, you will, in turn, change everyone around you and they will in turn, change everyone around them. Eventually, there will be no one in a community not touched. Something changes in the whole matrix of experience.

Fulfillment: A deep, personal sense of satisfaction comes from finding your purpose and making things happen in life that fulfills that purpose. Throughout the networlding process we receive fulfillment from our exchanges individually and even greater satisfaction from the awareness that we are making a difference for the people we are benefiting through our exchanges. Fulfillment offers us a panoramic view of the literally thousands of conversations we have with others throughout our lifetime and gives us a gauge that measures the degree of satisfaction we feel we are achieving. Celebrating small successes is a big part of this.

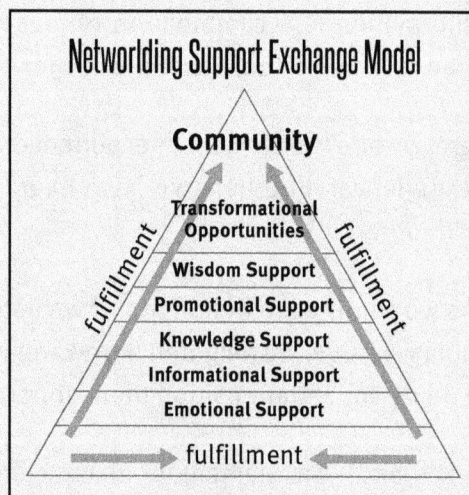

Networlding Support Exchange Model

Community

fulfillment

Transformational Opportunities

Wisdom Support

Promotional Support

Knowledge Support

Informational Support

Emotional Support

fulfillment

(The) Seven Steps of Networlding

1. **Establish a Values-Rich Foundation.** Identify your top values. Discover linkages to company values and goals.

2. **Make Connections for Your Primary.** Circle Identify who is currently in your Primary Circle and why.

3. **Expand Your Circles.** Identify and connect with new people who have similar and complimentary values.

4. **Initiate Exchanging Relationships.** Develop relationships more effectively by finding out what matters to others.

5. **Grow and Nurture Relationships.** Develop relationships with Primary Networlding Partners using The Networlding Support Exchange Model

6. **Co-create Opportunities.** Create transformational opportunities through continuous exchanges.

7. **Recreate Your Networld.** Achieve your goals: constantly reassess and expand relationships that align with your values.

"Grow Your Primary Power Circle"

Find and grow your Networlding Power Circle at this event.

	1
Name of Partner	
Company	Title
Phone	Email

Top 3 Values

_____

_____

_____

Top 3 Strengths

_____

_____

_____

2

Name of Partner	
Company	Title
Phone	Email

Top 3 Values

_____

_____

_____

Top 3 Strengths

_____

_____

_____

3

Name of Partner	
Company	Title
Phone	Email

Top 3 Values

_____

_____

_____

Top 3 Strengths

_____

_____

_____

4

Name of Partner	
Company	Title
Phone	Email

Top 3 Values

_____

_____

_____

Top 3 Strengths

_____

_____

_____

5

Name of Partner	
Company	Title
Phone	Email

Top 3 Values

_____

_____

_____

Top 3 Strengths

_____

_____

_____

6

Name of Partner	
Company	Title
Phone	Email

Top 3 Values

_____
_____
_____

Top 3 Strengths

_____
_____
_____

7

Name of Partner	
Company	Title
Phone	Email

Top 3 Values

_____
_____
_____

Top 3 Strengths

_____
_____
_____

8

Name of Partner	
Company	Title
Phone	Email

Top 3 Values

_____

_____

_____

Top 3 Strengths

_____

_____

_____

7

Name of Partner	
Company	Title
Phone	Email

Top 3 Values

_____

_____

_____

Top 3 Strengths

_____

_____

_____

A P P E N D I X E
Networlding Yearly Action Plan

Use this yearly calendar to help you organize your thoughts about the people you've connected with each month and how you will follow up on any action items that may have come as a result of building your primary circle.

January

Great people I have met to follow up with:

_____

_____

_____

Great organizations I have attended events at and plan to join:

_____

_____

_____

Great organizations I would like to attend events at in the future:

_____

_____

_____

Great tradeshows I will attend:

_____

_____

_____

Great referrals I have received:

_____

_____

_____

February:

Great people I have met to follow up with:

_____

_____

_____

Great organizations I have attended events at and plan to join:

_____

_____

_____

Great organizations I would like to attend events at in the future:

_____

_____

_____

Great tradeshows I will attend:

_____

_____

_____

Great referrals I have received:

_____

_____

_____

March:

Great people I have met to follow up with:

_____

_____

_____

Great organizations I have attended events at and plan to join:

_____

_____

_____

Great organizations I would like to attend events at in the future:

_____

_____

_____

Great tradeshows I will attend:

_____

_____

_____

Great referrals I have received:

_____

_____

_____

April:

Great people I have met to follow up with:

_____

_____

_____

Great organizations I have attended events at and plan to join:

_____

_____

_____

Great organizations I would like to attend events at in the future:

_____

_____

_____

Great tradeshows I will attend:

_____

_____

_____

Great referrals I have received:

_____

_____

_____

May:

Great people I have met to follow up with:

_____

_____

_____

Great organizations I have attended events at and plan to join:

_____

_____

_____

Great organizations I would like to attend events at in the future:

_____

_____

_____

Great tradeshows I will attend:

_____

_____

_____

Great referrals I have received:

_____

_____

_____

NETWORLDING YEARLY ACTION PLAN

June:

Great people I have met to follow up with:

_____

_____

_____

Great organizations I have attended events at and plan to join:

_____

_____

_____

Great organizations I would like to attend events at in the future:

_____

_____

_____

Great tradeshows I will attend:

_____

_____

_____

Great referrals I have received:

_____

_____

_____

TEEN LEADERSHIP NETWORKING GUIDEBOOK **79**

July:

Great people I have met to follow up with:

_____

_____

_____

Great organizations I have attended events at and plan to join:

_____

_____

_____

Great organizations I would like to attend events at in the future:

_____

_____

_____

Great tradeshows I will attend:

_____

_____

_____

Great referrals I have received:

_____

_____

_____

August:

Great people I have met to follow up with:

_____

_____

_____

Great organizations I have attended events at and plan to join:

_____

_____

_____

Great organizations I would like to attend events at in the future:

_____

_____

_____

Great tradeshows I will attend:

_____

_____

_____

Great referrals I have received:

_____

_____

_____

September:

Great people I have met to follow up with:

_____

_____

_____

Great organizations I have attended events at and plan to join:

_____

_____

_____

Great organizations I would like to attend events at in the future:

_____

_____

_____

Great tradeshows I will attend:

_____

_____

_____

Great referrals I have received:

_____

_____

_____

October:

Great people I have met to follow up with:

_____

_____

_____

Great organizations I have attended events at and plan to join:

_____

_____

_____

Great organizations I would like to attend events at in the future:

_____

_____

_____

Great tradeshows I will attend:

_____

_____

_____

Great referrals I have received:

_____

_____

_____

November:

Great people I have met to follow up with:

_____

_____

_____

Great organizations I have attended events at and plan to join:

_____

_____

_____

Great organizations I would like to attend events at in the future:

_____

_____

_____

Great tradeshows I will attend:

_____

_____

_____

Great referrals I have received:

_____

_____

_____

December:

Great people I have met to follow up with:

_____

_____

_____

Great organizations I have attended events at and plan to join:

_____

_____

_____

Great organizations I would like to attend events at in the future:

_____

_____

_____

Great tradeshows I will attend:

_____

_____

_____

Great referrals I have received:

_____

_____

_____

APPENDIX F
Journal

Date _____

_____

_____

_____

_____

_____

_____

_____

_____

_____

_____

_____

_____

_____

_____

_____

JOURNAL

Date _____

_____

_____

_____

_____

_____

_____

_____

_____

Date _____

_____

_____

_____

_____

_____

_____

_____

_____

_____

JOURNAL

Date _____

_____
_____
_____
_____
_____
_____
_____
_____

Date _____

_____
_____
_____
_____
_____
_____
_____
_____
_____
_____

JOURNAL

Date _____

_____

_____

_____

_____

_____

_____

_____

_____

Date _____

_____

_____

_____

_____

_____

_____

_____

_____

_____

Date _____

_____

_____

_____

_____

_____

_____

_____

_____

_____

Date _____

_____

_____

_____

_____

_____

_____

_____

_____

_____

JOURNAL

Date _____

_____
_____
_____
_____
_____
_____
_____
_____
_____

Date _____

_____
_____
_____
_____
_____
_____
_____
_____
_____

Date _____

_____

_____

_____

_____

_____

_____

_____

_____

_____

Date _____

_____

_____

_____

_____

_____

_____

_____

_____

_____

_____

JOURNAL

Date _____

_____
_____
_____
_____
_____
_____
_____
_____
_____
_____

Date _____

_____
_____
_____
_____
_____
_____
_____
_____
_____
_____
_____

Date _____

_____

_____

_____

_____

_____

_____

_____

_____

Date _____

_____

_____

_____

_____

_____

_____

_____

_____

_____

JOURNAL

Date _____

_____
_____
_____
_____
_____
_____
_____
_____
_____
_____

Date _____

_____
_____
_____
_____
_____
_____
_____
_____
_____
_____

Date _____

_____

_____

_____

_____

_____

_____

_____

_____

Date _____

_____

_____

_____

_____

_____

_____

_____

_____

_____

JOURNAL

Date _____

_____

_____

_____

_____

_____

_____

_____

_____

Date _____

_____

_____

_____

_____

_____

_____

_____

_____

Date _____

_____

_____

_____

_____

_____

_____

_____

_____

_____

Date _____

_____

_____

_____

_____

_____

_____

_____

_____

_____

JOURNAL

Date _____

_____
_____
_____
_____
_____
_____
_____
_____
_____
_____

Date _____

_____
_____
_____
_____
_____
_____
_____
_____
_____
_____

Date _____

_____

_____

_____

_____

_____

_____

_____

_____

_____

_____

Date _____

_____

_____

_____

_____

_____

_____

_____

_____

_____

_____

JOURNAL

Date _____

_____

_____

_____

_____

_____

_____

_____

_____

Date _____

_____

_____

_____

_____

_____

_____

_____

_____

101 GREAT TIPS

for Building Relationships and Opportunities in the Age of the Network

Helping You Build Better Business Faster
www.networlding.com

101 Ways to Networld Tips Booklet

Welcome. This booklet is designed to help you become successful no matter what the economy is doing, but it is even more powerful in tough times. We're sure you will benefit from the strategies here that represent years of research and development. They're practical; they're easy; they can be implemented quickly, and best of all, they work!

Fundamentals

1. Become a Networlder. A Networlder, unlike a networker, has 10 or fewer key people they consider partners. These partners are participants in regular exchanges of emotional support, information, knowledge, promotional support, as well as leads and referrals for new business or career opportunities. The focus of Networlding is on mutually beneficial exchanges with like-minded and like-valued people. The great thing about Networlding partnerships is that they are fun and get results three to five times as fast as traditional networking relationships.

2. Create a Primary Circle. We all have networks. We just don't necessarily realize it, and we spend most of our time with a few people. Networlding is about becoming aware of our network and consciously creating exchanges with a few people who become our Networlding partners in a primary circle. Social science research states that we can't communicate regularly with more than 15 people. Therefore, we have found Primary circles are no larger than 10 people.

3. Initially, you only need one Networlding partner in your Primary Circle. In an extensive study we did with 200 executives, we discovered that the majority of people connect with only five Networlding partners once a month, every month. This means that even one person with whom you share similar or complementary values and who is ready, willing and able to become a Networlding partner, can create a whole new world of opportunities for you and you for them.

4. Find Networlding influencers for your Primary Circle. We define Networlding influencers as people who know how to influence and are ready, willing and able to do so for you and others with whom they Networld. For example, you might know people who are in your industry who are highly influential but are not Networlding influencers because they keep their power to themselves.

5. Put others in Secondary and Tertiary Circles. Again, whether you consciously do this or not, some people will fall into your secondary or tertiary circles. People who might go in a secondary circle are those who are not, right now, ready, willing or able to exchange with you once a month. These are people, however, with whom you should stay in contact with and connect every three months. Tertiary circles are for almost everyone else, because you never know who might become a good partner later and vice versa. This is especially true for LinkedIn, because as you build your first connections on LinkedIn, you will develop secondary and tertiary networks.

6. Become a Networlding influencer. You can be someone who is not at the top of your field, but because you are willing to practice influencing—connecting people together who have not yet met but who should meet—and you can quickly become a top influencer, creating many opportunities for yourself.

7. Spend 80 percent of your relationship building time with your Primary Circle. We know this is counterintuitive but once you have found those 10 or fewer great Networlding partners, spend the majority of your time focused on your partners and your "collective" gain. This will make all the difference in achieving better business opportunities, faster. I call it the Power-of-Ten. Of course, that doesn't mean you can't have a large secondary or even tertiary networks as evidenced on LinkedIn, but there can never be very many that form a close knit alliance and co-create with you.

8. Treat each person you meet with uncompromising respect. Networlders are zealots of respect and integrity. They are like the knights in King Arthur's Roundtable. They care about creating relationships of honor.

9. Be proactive rather than reactive. Reactive people wait for a request to refer someone; proactive people are out there creating opportunities for you. These are people who will put you in a primary position in their networks and will actively work to find you new opportunities. Do the same for them.

10. Follow up promptly after face-to-face meetings. Email or call quality contacts you meet at networking gatherings promptly after an event to remind them of your initial meeting. You can even include Twitter and LinkedIn when you reach out. Reserve Facebook for close and personal contacts. Let them know you enjoyed meeting them. Focus on the appreciation you have for the original meeting and mention that you would like to stay connected. This is not a time to "sell" your services or products, but rather, a time to grow and deepen the connection around the relationship.

11. Stay in touch with your Networlding connections. Build rapport and follow them on Twitter, connect on LinkedIn and subscribe to their blogs. Maintain regular phone contact and email with information of value such as upcoming events or groups or important industry happenings.

12. Develop relationships with government representatives. These individuals can help access grants and other opportunities, such as government contracts and awards. Each state has reps on the city, state and federal level that serve businesses of all sizes.

13. Grab a pen. Bring back the art of good written communication by writing thank you notes to all your old and new contacts. Read trade journals in your industry. Find people who interest you and write to them using personalized note cards. Include an article from the Web or from a magazine with a handwritten note at the top saying something like, "FYI, George. Thought you would benefit from reading this article! Warmly, Melissa"

14. Become a resource for others. A technique for gaining visibility and credibility is to write or email editors of periodicals, advises a public relations expert. Contact reporters who write about your field and offer yourself as a resource for additional articles. Whatever can be done to make a reporter's job easier is usually greatly appreciated. If you have an opinion that is contrary or complementary to something you read in a column, take action quickly and email your comments to that columnist. This worked for me when someone sent me an article written by a reporter for The Wall Street Journal. Not only did I get into the journal, but I am now used as a regular resource for ongoing articles around the subject of networking as well as just for general business articles. Position yourself as a resource for others on Twitter too by sharing links.

15. Understand you have more to give than you think. Many people say, "I can't network because I have nothing to give!" However, master networkers realize that initially, there are many things they can exchange in addition to leads and referrals; for example, information obtained through regular reading and daily exchanges with others is a good place to start developing opportunities that will lead to referrals. Google Plus, Twitter, Facebook business pages and content curation tools (Scoop.it and Storify.com) are excellent ways of exchanging information. You can also connect people to other great Networlders. Tap in your LinkedIn network, as it allows you request an introduction to someone out of your network through a mutual connection, or choose to make a formal introudction. The real power, as Malcolm Gladwell confirms in his best-selling book, *The Tipping Point*, is in being the "connector" between two great people. EVERYONE can do that! Become a connector today!

16. Realize that Networlding is a long-term relationship. What you can't give today, you would be surprised to find you can give tomorrow. Your intent to deliver is really what matters. As a proactive networker you will find that you can create opportunities for your referral sources as you build a circle of high quality, not high quantity relationships.

17. Create three top success stories. Use these stories to build credibility with your contacts. If you have trouble creating your own stories, ask a colleague to interview you and write it for you and then, if you want, pay them something for the effort, or treat them to lunch or dinner. Another choice is to get someone with a writing background to help you and exchange some of your time for theirs. No matter what, it is good to have a written account that showcases the value proposition you can bring to your career or for new business opportunities. With so many great journalism students out of work today, you can give them a wonderful opportunity to keep their skills sharpened by writing your success stories.

18. Become a *collaborative* rather than a *guerilla* strategist. With the guerilla, the emphasis is on elimination through conquest. On the other hand, the collaborative strategist emphasizes cooperation in a joint effort. The goal is shared gain. Collaboration is not only more practical, but a choice that offers the biggest win.

19. Help people feel wanted. Recognize that most people want attention. Search for that uniqueness in others. Help them to feel significant. Do this by finding just one or two things about what they have said that you find most beneficial to you. Disclose your thoughts in a blog post, mention them on Twitter and/or with them personally.

20. Take action. It's not what you say, but what you do about what you say that makes the difference. There will be people who will tell you they will do many things for you, but watch out. Wait to see if they follow through on small things to know whether to trust them to follow through on bigger things.

21. Look at what contacts have done in the past. Find out what things they have completed and what long-term professional relationships they have. If they are constantly changing relationships, count on them exhibiting similar behavior with you.

22. Don't be afraid to move on to others who would be better Networlders. I constantly find the most successful people are those who can say "No" most often. This qualification process will help you build a network of "exchangers" rather than "takers."

23. Create a Networlding plan, then work it. Keep going back to your plan to adapt it to the results you are getting. Then re-plan the future, and adjust your projections. As you become more accurate at projecting, you will build skills in visualizing and implementing. Integrate a social media strategy calendar in your plan so you continue to expand your presence on the web.

24. Set realistic goals. If your goals are not realistic, they are just dreams, not goals. They should be aggressive enough for you to feel a sense of accomplishment by achieving them, but not unrealistic. A goal should be a challenge, not a chore.

25. Find a mentor. Mentors are available today through a number of organizations. One very powerful person I know put it this way: "I saw a young woman I had known for years at an event I was speaking at recently. She came up to me and told me that she appreciated me being her mentor for a number of years. I was surprised. I did not think of myself as her mentor and told her that if she had made that request I would have been happy to play an even stronger role in her life." The morale of this story is ask someone today to be your mentor. You will be surprised by the results. I have found that with hundreds of people to whom I have recommended this one strategy, they have reaped rewards of relationships they never thought possible. Don't be afraid to ask. Most successful people, surprisingly so, do want to help others. If you want, rather than by asking someone directly, ask people you trust if they know of someone who would "want" to be a mentor. This way you won't have to experience rejection, only the acceptance of someone who really wants to mentor.

26. Think Big! Why? It challenges you. This top-line thinking helps you get twice the results with half the effort by focusing on the quality of your contacts rather than the quantity. Each day offers new opportunities to get better results through strategic networking.

27. Study and model the successful Networlders. Treat all people as potential partners in networking. Your short-term objectives will keep changing whereas your long-term ones will remain stable.

28. Give yourself time. The saying goes. "It takes 21 days to form a habit." I prefer to give myself a year rather than days or months to develop new habits; you also have a better chance to sticking to them if you falter at times throughout the year. The real assessment of your success becomes whether you stuck with your new behavior for the majority of the year. With each new year, add a new level of performance to your Networlding and watch your network and the rewards of your efforts increase dramatically. Networlding has an exponential rather than an incremental growth. Take it seriously and your life will get easier, more fun and more rewarding for all involved. Time will also, unlike with networking, be on your side. You will find you are doing less and making more and more and more.

29. Give yourself permission to improve. Fact: your Networlding skills will improve over time if you keep challenging yourself to improve.

30. Uncovering the perceived value of your relationships requires you to create mutually beneficial exchanges. It will probably be something different for different people in your network. Ask those in your network how you can support them.

31. Before you call someone without an introduction from someone who knows the person you want to meet, ask yourself, "Who do I know who might know this person?" In this new age of connection, we have to go through fewer and fewer people to get introductions. Do your research on LinkedIn: see if you have a mutual connection that you can request an introduction from.

32. Focus on your connections and how you can help them. You only need a few people with whom you are growing deeper professional relationships to focus on monthly. In fact, the average executive has only about five people he or she keeps in regular contact with monthly. Therefore spend more time thinking about supporting fewer people. This attention will help your leverage the power of your network to, in turn, respond to your needs as one of their select few.

33. Meet new connections through the power of a good introduction. Keep making requests to those in your network to meet other select influencers in your industry and in your organization. Always look for the opportunity to help introduce others also. It's all about connection and introduction with a focus on adding value by finding out how you can support everyone with whom you connect. Investigate your LinkedIn network to find who is in your current, secondary and tertiary network, and read their profiles to find if you have mutual interests.

34. Share your knowledge. Offer those in your network a preview of your skills and talents. They will be able to then use what you have to offer in exchange for support you are seeking. Showcase your talent on social networks when appropriate.

35. Become an active listener. Listen for understanding versus listening for information. Your attention to your Networlding partner's needs and interests will help you create opportunities that can lead to even more and better opportunities for you in your networking exchanges.

36. Stay open to new ideas. Appreciate the new information or different way of looking at things your network partners offer. Even if you don't agree with them, respect their opinions. Successful networking comes from being open to the different viewpoints and ideas others share.

37. Keep asking questions. When you do the asking you can lead the conversation toward the most successful outcome and that outcome should be about both you and your Networlding partners gaining value from a networking exchange. Questions also keep both parties participating. 38. Create a list of the best questions for generating conversation. Great questions set the stage for great answers. Great answers inspire. Think of the best questions you can ask to start great conversation and exchanges. For example, if there is one thing you would want to do if this was the best year of your life, what would you do?

39. Compliment your network partners. Always make a point of recognizing and calling attention to the value you got from networking exchanges with your partners.

40. Create a balanced networking exchange. Life's lessons keep bringing us back to this truth. You don't benefit in the end when you take much more than you give. The same if also true when you give much more than you take.

41. Make your final words in your Networlding exchanges be, "What can I do for you or How can I support you?" This is the opposite of "What's in it for me?" Statements of support create reciprocal statements which is the heart of ongoing exchanges: the necessary element to any long-term, mutually beneficial relationship.

42. Stay genuine. Being prepared is great, but without sincerity, you have nothing. When you are genuine and sincere, you will attract people to you who naturally want to help you. Become interested in others. Find out what matters most to them and then center your conversations around their priorities. Of course, you should also share your priorities and Networld with those who care what matters to you as much as they care about what matters to them.

43. Ask for what you want. If you don't ask for what you want, you won't get it. There is nothing wrong with asking for what you want as long as you intend to help your partners get what they want. Remember, first you need to ask them what they want and then, if your partners don't ask you, tell them what it is that you want.

Leverage

44. Leverage your relationships. This means to co-create opportunities that offer the biggest win for the greatest number of people. Project collaborations, strategic alliances and partnering opportunities are all examples of ways to leverage relationships for maximum gain. That's what I did when I asked Jocelyn Carter-Miller, Chief Marketing Officer of Office Depot, to write my seventh book with me. Jocelyn benefited from the opportunity to publish a good book, and I gained a great colleague, friend and new business partner. The book also became a top seller, so we both gained in the exchange. The benefits today continue every year. Through Jocelyn I met Larry Mohl who is the head of five "centers of excellence" for American Express and we became partners. Now I am working on a new book with Larry that focuses on building networks within organizations today.

45. Balance your requests for potential business or new career opportunities with information, knowledge and promotional support of others. The other useful and powerful exchanges of information, knowledge and the promotion of others are like the kindling wood that will ignite the fire of new opportunities.

46. Meet face-to-face at least once a month with those in your primary circle. In the beginning stages of a networking relationship there is no substitute for one-on-one meetings. Those who are your top connections (of 10 or fewer) are very important. Meet with them at least once a month for an hour face-to-face.

47. Always look for new Primary Circle Partners. Primary Circle Partners come and go for many reasons — needs change, you move, etc.; therefore, keep developing opportunities to meet potential future partners and keep looking for ways to make an initial connection to begin a relationship.

48. Develop empathy for your connections. The ability to enter your network partner's world and see it through his or her eyes creates the foundation of a successful relationship.

49. Overcome rejection in networking by getting out your feelings as soon as possible. Write your experiences in a journal when you have a quiet moment. Indicate what happened. What was it that particularly bothered you? How did you feel? What will you say or do differently if a similar experience occurs in the future? Write down how you would take a more confident and powerful approach to handle similar situations in the future.

50. Create a statement that tells others what is unique about you with the emphasis of how you help others. Do you specialize in a particular market niche (e.g. healthcare, finance, telecommunications)? Have you created a new way of solving particular business problems? Declare it – write in a blog post.

51. The only way to overcome the fear of networking is to practice it regularly. Just like overcoming any kind of fear, you must face it and work continually to overcome it. If you need to take a friend with you, do so. A good way to overcome the fear of networking at public events is to assist with the registration, for example or join a greeter committee where you play the host rather than one of the attendees.

52. Act like a host rather than a guest. This gives you power to approach people, focusing on their needs, helping you forget your fears.

53. Call people showcased in magazines who have special interests similar to yours. One of the best for instance, has the email addresses of the people they showcase in their articles. Email these people when you are genuinely moved by something they said. Share your interests and something about yourself. Many successful networkers have met industry leaders this way and their relationships have lead to many opportunities that benefited them both.

54. Try out new organizations before joining. Call them. Ask to attend one of their most well-attended meetings. Also ask to speak to someone in charge of new membership. This person knows the top networkers in the organization. Ask to sit with someone in the organization who likes to "show prospective members around." This opportunity can lead to much more than if you just attended without knowing anyone.

55. Check local publications, online and off, to find good networking events. Ask your colleagues and those in your network (and social media networks) for the best places to network. Many top cities now have people who report and assess the best places to network.

56. Make a plan for attending an event and focus on quality instead of quantity. Get prepared for an event. Plan to meet just a couple of people. The more preparation you have the better.

57. Always have your business cards handy. This might seem like a simple rule of thumb when it comes to networking, but most of us forget to bring a small stack of cards with us wherever we go.

58. Follow-up with people you have committed to following up within 24 hours. You will establish yourself as a respected networker by keeping to this one commitment. Even if you can't provide the kind of support someone you met is looking for, be honest. Your candor will take you much further in networking success and will provide you with the kind of ongoing support you need in today's networked economy.

59. Bring someone with you to a networking event. One of the ways to Networld effectively is to go with someone who can introduce you to people he or she meets separately and vice versa. Also, if you are like the 50% of people who are shy, this strategy will help put you at ease.

60. Read key industry papers and online newsletters that offer insight on industry influencers. Keep looking for people you want to meet who are leaders in your industry and also in complementary industries. Publications that offer stories on leaders and lists of top influencers can be especially beneficial.

61. Find out how other people like to stay in touch. Adjust your communications with them. For example, if your Networlding partner prefers to be contacted by email, use that method of connection. You will get much further in the relationship faster. Search their social networks too to see where they are most active.

62. Be creative when thinking of people to contact. Start with people who really like you and brainstorm with them. Get them to give you a few names of people they really like but for one reason or another you have never met.

63. Set attainable goals. Keep your fear level down by setting attainable goals. For example, consider meeting just two people within the next month to do nothing more than exchange information.

64. Keep trying. Most of us go through an awkward stage at one time or another. If you create a big block of self-consciousness, you will only paralyze your progress. Instead, if you focus on the needs of others, you can often overlook your fear.

65. During exchanges ask your Networlding partner who they know in a specific industry. The more specific you are, the easier it is for others to help.

66. Ask for introductions to these people. If you don't ask, you will most likely not receive. Most people won't offer to make an introduction. The best thing you can do is to make the request to be introduced. Of course, this also means you need to offer introductions to those people you know whom others would like to meet.

67. Schedule return calls for a less hectic time of day. This will help you focus on the conversation and the important process of listening to your partners. Also, note we used the word "schedule" calls. We find the best way to have Networlding exchanges is to schedule calls so that both parties look at the exchange as a meeting that requires their full attention. It also works much better than trying to have sporadic, ad-hoc conversations of value.

68. Connect the unconnected. The research on human networks shows us that the real secret to creating a diverse, continuous and ever-growing flow of new business or career opportunities is to look for people who have yet to be connected. John may be looking for information about Company B and your colleague Susan whom John has yet to meet, works there. By linking the two together you create value for John and very likely

Susan who can benefit from knowing someone else who may very well become a new team player at her organization.

69. At the end of a Networlding Exchange, summarize what you exchanged. Summarizing what you exchanged—information, leads, referrals, advice, etc., helps both of you get a better understanding of any "to-do's" you might have decided to take on for one another's benefit. You keep focused on how to leverage the relationship from one of casual conversation to one of friendship coupled with supportive action.

70. Networld up and down. When you networld up you look for people who have influence in your industry or the community in general with whom you can offer more connections of value as you meet people who they don't know but should know. Networlding down is about being the mentor. Recently, Dave Ormesher of a great web design and development company called Closerlook, shared that he acquired a very large account with a company because he had befriended and mentored one of their sales people several years ago when everyone else would not give this person the time of day. Dave realizes that all people are worth the time it takes to let them know they are important and to provide them with guidance as to how to grow successfully.

71. Clean out your palm regularly or better yet, find out where everyone is regularly! On average, you will find half of those people in your database moved from where they were just months earlier. The web is a great way to find out where they have gone. Also, keep in touch with those people in your network who are super connectors. They are very likely to be great resources in helping you find people.

72. Keep a list of people you read about in your industry or anywhere that you admire and go over it regularly. In one group we run, we regularly ask them to bring in the names and information on three companies and three people they admire. With even 10 people attending these meetings we find we increase our awareness and connections 10-fold. We then share strategies for connecting with these people.

73. Mention people you want to meet in conversations. One Networlder kept mentioning the name of a president of a company she wanted to meet. Within a couple of weeks she found two people who had connections to people who knew the president. One was the CFO of the company, the other was the VP of Sales. She was then very cordially introduced to the president and is now doing great business with the company.

Etiquette

74. Maintain eye contact. There is nothing more annoying than people who don't look you in the eyes when they talk with you. Don't stare, but do maintain eye contact. This shows you care about what someone is saying.

75. Keep smiling. Yes, this is a simple tip, but one even we forget as our brows become furrowed after a full day of stress. Remind yourself to smile. It's the best door opener for Networlding.

76. Locate people who are standing alone. Networlders "include" others. Look for people standing alone and befriend them. Make an effort to help them get connected to others.

77. When calling someone, first ask if you have called at a convenient time. This question can help ensure that your conversation is heard and respected.

78. Send a thank you card or email not just to the person who gave you a referral or lead but if you can, from the original source. We call this "Honoring the Net." Ask your connection who was the originator of a connection. For example, I was in a major newspaper in an article on women entrepreneurs. I recommended four other women who were interviewed and also put in the article. In the original interview she recommended a person named Anne, who the reporter decided to do an article on next. Anne then recommended, as I did, three other image consultants. Anne made a point of sharing that it was I who created the first opportunity for her which evolved into opportunities for three more people. Each one of these new people should take the initiative to thank myself. Why? First of all, it is good etiquette. Second, it could also lead to other opportunities for myself, who is a resource for articles, to refer them directly.

Mastering Networlding

79. Become a business matchmaker. If you see someone who can benefit from meeting someone else, make an introduction.

80. Create a statement that tells others what you do in the most favorable way. For example, an accountant might say, "I help people start and maintain small businesses."

81. Use a sheet of colored paper to write down an action plan for the next three months. Put this sheet up somewhere where you can see it. Another option is to download the Networlding Planner from the networlding site at www.networlding.com. It's free and a practical way to keep focused on your goals.

82. Help your Networlding partners locate prospects for you by having regular exchanges where you share your latest Networlding stories. Keep the interest in Networlding with you alive by sharing your latest success stories. Who did you work with in the last month who appreciated your work, or what good results are you currently getting from a project you are working on or who did you meet that might be someone good to connect with your partner? The more you share these stories, the more connections you create.

83. Request referrals in one industry at a time. People will more likely remember this request.

84. Assume you will create great Networlding opportunities. Ok, so we are like other consultants who talk about the power of the mind to create your future, but it is true. Believing it so makes it more real and what do you get if you don't believe? We find that you get the opposite—nothing. Now, you might not be disappointed because you expected nothing and that is just what you got, but in our books we find that really dedicating yourself to believing in the tenant that great things will happen when you Networld, actually creates the result. Why? Because you have conversations about "possibility." You are, as Louis Pasteur once said, "helping chance favor the prepared mind." So, talk up possibility. Believe in it and then . . . make it happen! 85. Ask people regularly, "Who do you admire?" Ah, another great conversation opener and grower. Ask this question often. Networlding is all about relationships first, then success. We don't know about you, but the last think we want is lots of money and no friends to share it with. People who others admire are likely to be people you admire—people who can become good friends as well as people who might lead us to the best opportunities of our lives.

86. Suspend judgment when you meet someone new. We often find ourselves meeting people who, upon first glance, don't seem to have the wherewithal to exchange or just don't seem like the sharing type. However, we make it a rule to give each person the opportunity to exchange with us toward the possibility of partnership. I constantly mentor others toward becoming better partners. I see this as a way to teach the world through these people–how to be better at sharing

87. Get out of your own way. When a thought comes into your mind that is not supportive of your growth, remind yourself: you have a choice. You can digest it and then it becomes a part of you, or you can see it as a mere breeze and let it blow away, out from whence it came. Only supportive thoughts help you. All the rest are merely commentary that you can dismiss.

88. Assume you will meet great people at an event. Keep an open mind about this even if there are very few people attending. Over the last decade we have found that the best events are the smaller events where people get to know one another better. Keep in mind new comers provide unique opportunities to band together with future leaders. Befriend them early; they will appreciate the support and benefits will appear over the years.

89. Help organizations in your area start structured Networlding. I have been doing structured networking events for years, and found that they are much more effective for creating the space for all participants to connect and exchange. For example, I helped start what is called The Pink Slip Parties in Chicago. Rather than 400 plus people coming together to network with each other including recruiters and hiring companies, I recommended they start each person in a Power-of-Ten Networlding Circle where they were able to get support and exchange with one another. Each circle then became a support team with each participant going out to the large community to help locate opportunities for one another. People found new jobs much faster and of course, created new friendships at the same time.

90. When you are at an event, meet the speaker. Speakers are great people to meet as they usually are not only influential but good Networlders. They usually understand the importance of growing their connections. Therefore, while they are speaking, think of something they have said that was compelling to you. Write it down on the back of your business card along with a question. Hand this to them and ask to email them. This can be the start of a good Primary Circle Partnership or at least someone to put in your Secondary Circle.

91. Do MORE of LESS every day. Focus the majority of your efforts on accomplishing just those goals that carry the highest priority. We have found that spending time on the 20% of tasks that yield 80% of your results daily really moves you to getting better results with less effort.

92. Take time to play. Again, it may seem counter-intuitive, but play is a leveraging technique. In Networlding like networking, this can include playing golf, going to ball games, etc., but it can also include different activities. For example, I recently met a Networlding partner who was an executive at a large company, at The Art Institute in Chicago. My colleague Cheryl, with whom I worked at one time helping build Networlding communities, was now between jobs. Cheryl and I created a whole new level of connection as friends as we enjoyed a fun-filled day at the art museum. At the end of the day, we chatted about work and the results we achieved. To my surprise, Cheryl shared how successful my Networlding strategies had been with their communities, stating that out of 40 communities that were formed with 100 people, it was really the one community I recommended to form additional circles of 10 that took off. I might have never learned that my ideas had that impact had I not considered the fun side of work. It's always there; we just have to see it.

93. Even if you have only five minutes to talk with someone, take your time. Everyone deserves your attention. We have found many people, especially journalists, say things like, "I'm on deadline." We suggest saying, rather, "I only have a couple of minutes but I would love to hear what you have to say." Again, Networlding is about honoring people. As you honor so shall you be honored back!

94. Lighten up! If you Networld right, you should experience total success combined with great joy.

95. Good Networlding partners are everywhere. Look for partners everywhere. One Networlder meets most of her partners on planes. She makes it a point to fly first class whenever she can and the rest, as she says, is history.

96. Once you build a circle, PASS IT ON. Networlding is about learning, growing and most of all, sharing. If you share it, it will come back to you ten fold. Find someone in a local university who would love to be mentored on Networlding. Make sure you let the person you mentor know that they have an obligation. Once they receive the learning of Networlding, they too must pass it on. Think about it, if everyone you connected with shared these learning with others, then the world would be a better place for all as everyone you meet will understand how to exchange.

97. Start a Networlding Circle. Power-of-Ten Networlding Circles are spreading around the world. These support groups are to help people learn and practice Networlding. They are not a replacement for a Primary Circle but an addition to your Networld. They help you locate new Primary Circle partners while practicing the seven steps of Networlding.

98. Take time to pause. Take time to reflect on your connections. This time will help you make even deeper neural connections as to possibilities for you and your Networlding partners.

99. Be flexible with your goals. Networlding is about creating surprising opportunities that might actually change your goals. For instance, say you want to find a new piece of business in a particular industry or a new career. Then you meet a wonderful Networlding partner in a totally different industry and all of a sudden, you are now offered a new opportunity that you didn't expect. Be open to these new opportunities because it really is about your relationships first, opportunities second. In other words, ask yourself, would you rather work on a good opportunity with a great person or a great opportunity with people with whom you have no synergy?

100. Always revisit your plan. I can't count the number of times anymore that I see people who stay with a plan long after it is still working. My rule of thumb is that every six months you should revisit your plan and really ask yourself tough questions as to whether you should consider going with it anymore. It's a paradox. While you will be most successful focusing your plan and then working it until it starts to realize traction, it is also good to know when to quit on something and start fresh in a new direction.

101. Find the best resources and make them your partners. From the great web site developers we have that enable us to manage our site like a Word document daily (www.norvax.com) to organizations like Cameo Publications (www.cameopublications.com) that can help you from beginning to end, create your own books, newsletters and other great business publications.

BONUS SOCIAL MEDIA TIPS:

In today's world of web 2.0 and pervasive social media, Networlders understand the importance of networking through various social media platforms. Virtual relationships can facilitate the return you are looking for and social media has proven to be an effective medium. The 101 tips are applicable to social networking, and maintaining a Power-of-Ten circle presence on the web is achievable. Networlders have a keen eye for information exchange and concept introduction opportunities, and social media is a fertile ground for such activities.

102. If you do not have a LinkedIn, Google Plus, Facebook Business Page and Twitter account, we highly encourage you to obtain them. Create robust profiles. In fact, LinkedIn, a professional network, say users with complete profiles are 40 times more likely to receive opportunities through LinkedIn.

103. Start your own blog. A general rule of thumb reads that you should have at least 10 posts addressing different subjects prior to sharing your blog in order to enhance credibility to your effort. A blog enables your loyal friends and fans consistently connect to you in a fresh and robust manner. Your blog should be your cornerstone for social networking, because it is of your own making and free of outside influences.

104. Subscribe to blogs but be prudent with the number of blogs. How many will you actually read? Use a tool like Newswire, RSS feeds or Google Reader to manage your subscriptions and read at least one a day. Try to publish a thoughtful comment daily.

105. Join LinkedIn groups. While you can join up to 50 groups, it is more practical to participate in six to eight groups and make your association and contribution meaningful. There are many topics to choose from and aligning yourself with your field of interest and industry should be easy. Ask insightful questions and provide informed perspective in discussions.

106. Do not become lazy about welcoming new followers. Interaction is the name of the game. Do not get into the Auto Direct Message habit. Take the time to look at their profile and ask a question.

107. Manage your networks using a tool such as www.hootsuite.com where you can integrate multiple accounts and schedule tweets and updates. We understand you are busy, but avoid the temptation of utilizing automated "response" programs. If your participation in social media appears automated, your credibility will suffer. Provide for meaningful personal time in your daily schedule.

108. Curate content by choosing the best tweets, posts, articles and other information (including your own best) and assembling it in one place. Use www.storify.com (which is especially good for interviews) and www.scoop.it (arranges it in a gorgeous magazine format). You will be able to share them with your connections and establish yourself as a "go-to" person in your industry.

109. Participation in tweet chats through www.tweetchats.com is an effective way to gain entrance into a networking event that complements your background and perspective. Participation in tweetchats can elevate your social media presence through gaining followers who find your contributions to discussions worthy of their own personal investigation. Refrain from spamming the chats with self promotion links. Do a Google search of tweetchats to find what matches your industry and interests. If there are none, you may want to consider creating one and originating a chat. You might start one with your own Power-of-Ten circle and branch out as people to take notice.

110. Focus on transparency and authenticity in your social media endeavors. People can sense insincerity on the web as quickly as they take notice in person. Small personal comments can have a dramatic impact on relationships.

Review your Networlding plan regularly and remember, "It's always about people first, opportunities, second!"

I am always looking over my Networlding yearly, action plan. But what I focus on are the relationships I have with my primary circle and how they relate to the opportunities I am developing. I am honest with others I meet if, at this time, I cannot include them in my Primary Circle because I am tapped out. I also revisit my opportunities with my current, Primary Circle partners regularly. It makes all the differences in getting the resources and action strategies that leverage opportunities faster.

"When You Schmooze, You Lose," Says Julia Hubbel, Speaker, Trainer and Author.

To be able to Networld means following a wholly different set of guidelines and holding a positive, service-focused attitude. Julia Hubbel's new book sets forth ground rules, success techniques and easy ways to approach and get to know people when at a networking event. The following New Networking Ground Rules are adapted from her forthcoming book *When You Schmooze, You Lose; The Handbook for People Who Hate to Network*.

The New Networking Ground Rules are based on very different attitude about how to interact with people:

It's Not What's In It For Me, But What's In Me for You! This new attitude turns the tables on old-style networking. It means that we enter a room looking to make a difference, to be of service. It means that we know we have something of value to offer those in that room. It means that we understand that our needs will be taken care of along the way. And it puts us in charge. Instead of looking for something, feeling like we have to ask for help, we're looking for an opportunity to share our social capital. This means that we listen carefully to people, waiting for a chance to give them some assistance. How differently would you feel about networking with someone who felt this way about you? You'd really want to talk to this person! People will want to talk to you, too.

People who understand that networking is really about giving instead of getting are some of the most successful people you'll ever meet. They know that by giving generously because it's the right thing to do, they will achieve their goals. They operate unselfishly and are focused on other's needs first. When you realize how easy this is to do and how much benefit is to be gained by such an attitude, you'll want to live by the New Networking Ground Rules as well!

Ground Rule #1: **Exchanging Business Cards First Isn't a Good Idea!** Business cards are only a tiny snapshot of who we are – or think we are – in our business lives. It's too easy to make a snap judgment about someone based on their title, and either dismiss them or give them special importance based on what that tiny piece of paper tells us. With the exception of the formalities of some cultures, like the Japanese, I recommend that you find out more about who you're talking to first before you exchange cards. Find out where your mutual connections, values and interests are. Discover the personal connection first, then exchange cards – by the time you have traded cards, you'll know that you want to know the person, not the title, and the connection will have much more meaning and significance.

Ground Rule #2: **It's Not What You Say, It's What You Ask!** Are you worried about what you're going to say to people you meet? Whether your stories are going to come out right or if your mini-commercial will bomb?

Who cares? Put your attention on the other person, not you! The point is that when your focus is on asking the other person about his or her background and opinions, you're making it easy for them to talk. Learn about your conversational partner. You'll find yourself relaxing and enjoying the conversation because the onus is off you to be entertaining. As Melissa Giovagnoli says "listen to understand." Ask good journalistic questions and attend to the answers. People will experience you as a great conversationalist even though you're doing all the listening – and learning. Whether approaching a group or one person, come armed with good questions. With rare exception it will work and you'll find yourself fascinated by what you hear!

Ground Rule #3: **Discover Something Wonderful!** No matter who you're talking to, there is something interesting, even riveting about that person. Make it a point to try to find out what that is. Melissa advises to put aside your first impressions – when you can do this, the person's real value can come through. Ask lots of probing questions, and expect to find something surprising and different. I guarantee you that you will if you try hard enough- people are full of surprises. When we can get past our judgments and first impressions and focus on what other people have to offer; when you discover something wonderful, they will realize that they're special – and appreciate you very much for it.

Ground Rule #4: **Be Clear About Your Intent.** Melissa Giovagnoli and Jocelyn Carter-Miller describe the importance of intent in Networlding: "We use it to mean forming relationships and opportunities intentionally – being highly conscious about the underlying values, goals, and beliefs that drive you towards a specific relationship or opportunity. Your intent may be to obtain a specific job or to establish a certain type of business but it is also to know what beliefs and values are important to you as you pursue these goals."

Be very clear about why you're at a networking event. It doesn't matter whether your boss made you go or if you're trying to make friends in a new community. Take a few minutes and think carefully about these questions:

- Why am I attending this event?
- What do I have to offer people I might meet at this event?
- What do I need from people at this event?
- What are your ideal outcomes from this event?

Be very clear about what you want, what you expect, and what your motives are before you attend a networking event. People will know what you're about even if you're not clear.

Ground Rule #5: **Listen With An Intent to Serve.** This attitude takes networking/networlding to another level. I believe you should look for an opportunity to make a difference in that person's life. Whether it's a recommendation for a good restaurant, a referral to your network of friends, a job opportunity you know about or to set up an introduction to a friend, watch out for anything you can give to this person. The point is that the focus of your listening is completely on understanding their needs, hearing their meaning, and finding an opportunity to give something of value. Dr. Wayne Dyer says in *You'll See It When You Believe It*, "in a network the purpose is to give power away." In other words, the more you give, the more you get – directly or indirectly. This may go against conventional wisdom, but it works, and works remarkably well when it comes from genuine service-focused intention.

Searching for a way to be of service requires that you listen at all levels while at the same time thinking about what you have to offer. This places the focus completely on the other person and on what you can give. When you're in a position to give something—and we all are in that position—you have a lot of power to make someone else's life better. This is exhilarating—and it takes all the pressure off you to be entertaining, witty, or anything else you thought you had to be.

Ground Rule #6: **Tithe Your Social Capital.** Your social capital is immense. It's everyone your know in your life, and everything all those people have to offer. Your human capital, according to Dr. Wayne Baker (*Achieving Success Through Social Capital*), is everything you know: your book knowledge, life experiences, wisdom and know-how. But you don't have to be an expert, just know one. You don't have to have the knowledge, just know where to find it. And it doesn't have to be work-related. For example, if you've met someone who just moved to town, chances are they're looking for referrals to basic services– from a veterinarian to a good dentist. If you have good ones, recommend yours. It takes nothing for you to provide a phone and an address; chances are they're in your PDA or day-timer. And it means a great deal to a newcomer to get a good recommendation. That's an easy gift to give.

By *Tithing your Social Capital*...I mean that you look for a way to draw up on your resources to be of service to someone else. Just as we tithe to charities, I believe we should tithe from our resources to create opportunities for others.

What happens when you enter a networking event with a primary goal of tithing your social capital? First of all, you start out looking for opportunities to serve. People will be naturally drawn to you because that's the intention you're expressing. You'll automatically start asking good questions and listening carefully for ways to give something of value. And when you do, and do it freely, people will be surprised–and very grateful.

Ground Rule #7: **No Quid Pro Quo.** It is essential that when you give, you give without an expectation of getting back. Not from the person you're giving to or anyone else, for that matter. What you offer – whether it's a phone number to a cherished resource or the name of your family chiropractor – must be given without a demand, implied or stated, that something must be offered in return. Otherwise, it's not a gift. It's coercion. And people can tell the difference.

What I'm talking about is reciprocity. In *Achieving Success Through Social Capital*, Dr. Wayne Baker explains: "The principle of reciprocity explains why building social capital works: when you use your networks to contribute to others, others contribute to you."

There is an essential difference between offering something freely, and offering it with strings, especially when you give something of no value away in hopes of getting something of value in return. That's quid pro quo at its worst, and it's not what I'm advocating here.

Baker continues, "The misuse of the reciprocity principle, then, adds nothing to our fund of social capital; it doesn't create new opportunities."

Here's where we return to your real intention. If your intention is to be of service, and it's an authentic intent, then what you offer will be given freely and without strings, and others will sense that and feel free to accept. Does this mean that you shouldn't accept something in return? Not at all. It does mean, however, that your offering doesn't come with a built-in guilt load so that the recipient feels that he must give back.

Ground Rule #8: **Have a Pocket Story,** How many times have you initiated a conversation, asked questions, done your best to get things going and got no result? Sometimes people just don't want to talk. Maybe that is just how they feel or something is bothering them that has nothing to do with you. Sometimes, though, they might be intimidated by you, or intimidated by the fact that they don't know anything about you. In cases like this, it's helpful to have a quick short story to tell about yourself. Ideally, the story is a little self-deprecating, the "dunce hero" version of a tale, which makes people laugh and helps them to relax around you. It should be no more than two or three minutes long, allowing people to see you as a human being who makes mistakes. By doing this, you humanize yourself, and you invite people to get past any negative first impressions.

The most important thing about telling a story, especially when you're the "dunce hero," is that you cannot possibly be pretentious. When we're willing to let the curtain down a bit and invite people to laugh at our own foibles, we let people have access to our authentic selves. When you're telling a story, people get the real you, not your title, not your accomplishments. And the real you is the person whom they're trying to reach in order to decide if they want to establish a relationship. Melissa advises us to have success stories to express our capabilities, and this is crucial to helping others understand our skills. But I recommend that you have a Pocket Story, to let people experience the other side of you as well.

Ground Rule #9: **The Revelation Creates the Relationship,** When you choose to tell a Pocket Story, you create the opportunity for people to experience something surprising and different about you. I believe it's important to reveal something that allows others to see us as we are, not as we're trying to appear.

We work hard to look professional, in control, powerful, successful. What we forget is that this impression makes us more distant to many of those who would like to meet us, and

TEEN LEADERSHIP NETWORKING GUIDEBOOK **127**

whom we need to meet. Lee Glickstein, author of *Be Heard Now*, writes, "The hilarious secret of human nature is that nobody had it together, yet everybody pretends to have it together." The truth is that we're all so intent on looking polished and professional – because we think everyone else is so together – that we miss the opportunity to connect. My lesson was to learn to be a little more vulnerable in my speeches and during my networking. This made my heart stop the first few times I did it, but it quickly taught me that the fine art of revealing a little vulnerability went a long way towards opening the door to genuine friendships and business connections. I was afraid that by being vulnerable, by sharing something personal about my own failings or embarrassing situations, I'd turn people off. I couldn't have been more wrong. My learning to be vulnerable, I discovered that it wasn't a weakness. It was empowering, and led to much deeper personal connections.

Ground Rule #10: **The Gentle Art of Disengagement.** There are times at any networking event when you are going to find yourself in a conversation you wish to leave, whether it's because there is nothing in common or because of a time pressure. And sometimes our conversational partners might not make it easy for us to make our exit. Here are some basic tips on gently disengaging yourself from typical networking types. – The domineering networker is going to expect you to attend to his every word, but he respects goal orientation. You may have to interrupt him to say you have a deadline to meet, but once you have his attention, he'll respect your time needs and let you go. And forget about you immediately.

✓ The high-energy, storytelling, center of attention networker expects you to be hanging on to every word of her story, so try to get both of you to a larger audience where she can continue her tale and you can make your getaway. She will also forget you immediately as long as there are others paying attention to her.

✓ The quiet, focused, friendly networker is the most likely to want to stay with you, having made a friend and often creating what he feels is a safe haven from the crowds. You must gently explain that you have responsibilities to attend to, you enjoyed your time with him, are happy to get together later but must move on. Do this firmly, and you will be able to go, but you might have to repeat yourself to make your point. Don't wait to leave, they are likely to start another conversation to keep you there.

✓ The detail-oriented, careful observer who has decided that you are worthy of his audience may pose a real challenge. You must interrupt her, perhaps several times, (she won't be listening to you) and explain in clear, concise terms that you have to be somewhere at a specific time, you find the conversation fascinating but perhaps can reschedule (be prepared to set a time later). You may have to say this several times because she's waiting for you to finish so she can get back to her points. Be firm, be focused, and physically move away by shaking hands and leaving.

✓ The Suckerfish is the most challenging, for he attaches himself to your sleeve and won't let you move around on your own. He has decided that you are his friend for the entire event and it is like having a piece of luggage move with you everywhere you go. In this case you must be firm almost to the point of rudeness. State that you both have networking responsibilities, and in the worst cases, have a "savior" come get you for your "meeting." Sound dishonest? It is. But the next time you have one or two people tagging at your heels at a busy event because they're terrified of going off on their own, you'll wish you had a prearranged lifesaver as well.

Fear does terrible things to people. But you are at an event to get work done, and so are they. Be courteous. Be kind. Be direct. But break free and do what you came to do. It might just be the wakeup call they needed.

Whatever you do, be appreciative of the other person's feelings. You are always setting an example, so be cognizant of upholding Networlding principles in all your exchanges.

www.ingramcontent.com/pod-product-compliance
Lightning Source LLC
Chambersburg PA
CBHW051414200326
41520CB00023B/7224